CONTENTS

1)	Introduction to Daniel Defoe	1
2)	Introduction to Robinson Crusoe	14
3)	Textual Analysis	15
	Chapters 1 - 4	15
	Chapters 5 - 9	19
	Chapters 10 - 18	24
	Chapters 19 - 38	33
	Chapters 39 - 44	55
4)	Character Analyses	66
5)	Critical Commentary	72
6)	Essay Questions and Answers	75
7)	Bibliography	78

BRIGHT NOTES

ROBINSON CRUSOE BY DANIEL DEFOE

Intelligent Education

INFLUENCE PUBLISHERS

Nashville, Tennessee

BRIGHT NOTES: Robinson Crusoe
www.BrightNotes.com

No part of this publication may be used or reproduced in any manner whatsoever without written permission, except in the case of brief quotations in critical articles and reviews. For permissions, contact Influence Publishers http://www.influencepublishers.com.

ISBN: 978-1-645420-72-9 (Paperback)
ISBN: 978-1-645420-73-6 (eBook)

Published in accordance with the U.S. Copyright Office Orphan Works and Mass Digitization report of the register of copyrights, June 2015.

Originally published by Monarch Press.
Thomas A. Duff, 1966
2020 Edition published by Influence Publishers.

Interior design by Lapiz Digital Services. Cover Design by Thinkpen Designs.

Printed in the United States of America.

Library of Congress Cataloging-in-Publication Data forthcoming.
Names: Intelligent Education
Title: BRIGHT NOTES: Robinson Crusoe
Subject: STU004000 STUDY AIDS / Book Notes

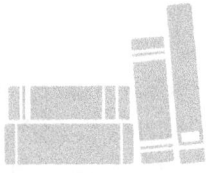

INTRODUCTION TO DANIEL DEFOE

INTRODUCTION

Daniel Defoe is best known as the author of *Robinson Crusoe*. However, his life encompassed such a diversity of activities that no single word such as "novelist" adequately describes him. His literary output was enormous, with some five hundred publications to his credit, but the few works of fiction were written late in his life. Propagandist and pamphleteer, novelist and reporter, Defoe also found time to write histories, biographies, travelogues and poetry. In addition to his literary activities, Defoe also pursued a number of other careers. He prided himself on his business ability and always maintained that he was primarily a merchant. For a number of years he also acted as a secret agent for Robert Harley, the Secretary of State. Very much involved with contemporary affairs, Defoe's writings, whether fictional, reportorial or polemical, reflect the interests and opinions of his times. For a fuller understanding of Defoe himself, it is therefore necessary to know something about his England.

HISTORICAL BACKGROUND: THE MONARCHS

During Defoe's lifetime (1660-1731), six monarchs reigned in England. The Stuart king, Charles II, was restored to the throne which had been vacant since his father's beheading twelve years before, in 1660. Charles II had considerably more tact than his ancestors and did not allow his personal preference for absolute rule and Roman Catholicism to offend the more democratic and Protestant susceptibilities of his subjects. His brother James II, who succeeded him in 1685, was less wise and openly avowed his Roman Catholicism. As a direct result of the birth of a son in 1688, the "Glorious Revolution" (so-called because it was brief and bloodless), replaced James by his elder, Protestant daughter, Mary and her husband William of Orange. They had no children and were succeeded by Mary's younger sister Anne in 1702. None of Anne's children survived her, so she was succeeded by a distant, Protestant relation, George I of Hanover, in 1714. His son, George II, ascended the throne in 1727.

HISTORICAL BACKGROUND: WAR WITH FRANCE

While Charles II and James II reigned, England maintained peaceful relations with Louis XIV's France. However, William III soon involved England in his lifelong feud with the French. Although peace was declared in 1697, war again broke out in 1701. This, the "war of the Spanish succession," continued until 1713. In both cases England was the victor.

HISTORICAL BACKGROUND: POLITICAL

The terms of the settlement by which William and Mary ascended the throne vacated by James II established that England would be a constitutional monarchy, governed by Parliament. Although the king remained in nominal control, his ministers now had more power than previously. The ministers were members of Parliament and they retained office only as long as they were able to control Parliament. Since no one man could be sure of the support of more than a few of the members of the House of Commons, several men who had similar ideas concerning the way in which the country should be run would join together. In this way political parties were formed. During Defoe's lifetime there were two parties, called the Whigs and the Tories. The Tories belonged to the upper classes, supported the supremacy of the Church of England and favored the restoration of the Stuart monarchy in the person of James II's son, the "Old Pretender." The Whigs, on the other hand, often belonged to the middle class, favored toleration for the various Protestant groups and supported the Hanoverian dynasty. Between the two extremes there were many moderates. All those Protestants who did not belong to the Church of England (also known as the Anglican Church) were called Dissenters. Dissenters were not permitted to hold office, but many of them did by attending the Anglican Church occasionally. Defoe was against this practice of "occasional conformity" and wrote a pamphlet attacking it.

HISTORICAL BACKGROUND: SCOTLAND

During the period of the Stuart monarchs, Scotland and England were allied because they shared the same king. James I of England was also James VI of Scotland. With the overthrow of the Stuart dynasty in 1688, it became apparent that closer political ties with Scotland would have to be established. Therefore, the two countries were legally unified by the Act of Union in 1707. Defoe was quite active in furthering this treaty which brought England and Scotland together.

HISTORICAL BACKGROUND: TRADE AND THE MIDDLE CLASS

The seventeenth and eighteenth centuries witnessed the rise of the middle class to a position of power and prestige. Their influence would cause England, in the nineteenth century, to be known as a "nation of shopkeepers." Trade was occupying a more important position in the nation's economy than it ever had before. With ability, luck and a few influential friends, a young man could rise to be a great merchant. He might even marry the daughter of a duke or become a member of the nobility himself. Daniel Defoe undoubtedly had ambitions of this nature.

DEFOE'S CHILDHOOD

Born sometime in 1660 (the year of Charles II's restoration to the throne), Defoe was the son of a Dissenting tradesman. His father, James Foe, did not believe in infant baptism, so we have no record of Defoe's birth. (Defoe added the aristocratic prefix "De" to his family name toward the end of the century.) Born and brought up in London, Defoe spent the greater part of his life in or near it. He was probably only five years old when the great plague of 1665-66 broke out, but he remembered what he was told about the tragic epidemic and wrote the effective *Journal of the Plague Year* in 1722. In September of 1666 occurred the great fire of London which destroyed most of the old city, but stopped short a few blocks from the Foe home. Defoe went to schools run by the Dissenters, and the education he acquired here stressed subjects such as history and geography, rather than the Latin and Greek which predominated at the universities of Oxford and Cambridge (which were open only to Anglicans). He originally intended to study for the Presbyterian ministry, but decided that he was unsuitable and instead prepared himself to become a merchant, like his father.

THE YOUNG MERCHANT

By 1683, Defoe was established as a merchant, dealing primarily in haberdashery. The following year, he married Mary Tuffley, whose father was moderately wealthy. Although in later years Defoe was able to give sound advice to young men beginning business careers, he never followed his own precepts. He persistently overreached himself in financial matters, becoming involved in more risky and ultimately unsuccessful ventures than profitable undertakings. He was also involved in a number of lawsuits. Biographers differ on how guilty he was of the many charges of dishonesty leveled against him, but it is unlikely that he was completely innocent in all cases. Defoe also suffered some severe financial losses as a direct result of King William's war with the French, when ships he insured were captured by the enemy. As a result of bad luck, poor judgment and perhaps dishonesty, Defoe found himself unable to pay his bills and was declared a bankrupt in 1692. Within ten years, the greater part of the debt had been repaid, but Defoe was forever after haunted by the threat of debtors' prison.

POLITICAL ASSOCIATIONS

Defoe, as a good Dissenter, feared the consequences of a Roman Catholic sovereign. He therefore supported the uprising of 1685 (which attempted to replace James II by Charles II's natural son, the Protestant Duke of Monmouth) but escaped punishment when the revolt failed. Defoe was firmer in his support of

William III; one of his first political pamphlets, "A Letter to a Dissenter from his friend at the Hague" (published anonymously in the summer of 1688), openly criticized James II's policies. Welcoming William III's arrival in England, Defoe soon made himself useful to the new monarch and his ministers, and was rewarded by several minor government positions. By the end of the century, Defoe was writing pamphlets fairly regularly in support of William's policies. In 1701, Defoe published a satirical poem, "The True-Born Englishman", as an answer to critics who complained that England was being overrun by "foreigners" that is, by William III's Dutch friends and advisers. The point of the extremely popular poem was that the ancestors of all Englishmen were foreigners once. During the same year, Defoe did an even greater service for William in writing "Legion's Memorial" to the House of Commons. Parliament, instead of voting military supplies to support William's war, had been bickering about unimportant matters. Defoe's pamphlet, which he personally gave to Robert Harley, then Speaker of the House, warned Commons that Parliament should serve the people, and if it did not, the people could overthrow it.

FALL FROM FAVOR

Defoe felt that his position was now secure. Unfortunately, William III died on March 8, 1702. His sister-in-law, Anne, favored the extreme Tories, so Defoe, as a Dissenting Whig could hope for no more royal favors. At the end of this year, angered by sermons and speeches advocating religious persecution of all Dissenting sects, Defoe anonymously published a pamphlet called "The Shortest Way" with the Dissenters. Written tongue-in-cheek, "The Shortest Way" advocated extreme repressive measures against the Dissenters, such as hanging and banishment. Unfortunately, the sermons Defoe was satirizing used language that was just as violent, and for a while everyone thought that the anonymous author was sincere. When it was found that Defoe was the author, both the Dissenters and the Tories were extremely angry with him and the Tories decided that he should be punished. Accordingly, Defoe was charged with writing a seditious libel and sentenced to the extremely severe punishment of standing three times in the pillory, paying a fine, and remaining in prison for an indefinite time. Defoe's Whig friends managed affairs so that, while Defoe had to stand in the pillory (a T-shaped construction with holes for the head and hands) his public exposure turned into a personal triumph. Instead of jeering and throwing things at him, the crowd cheered and bought copies of his latest **satire**, "A Hymn to the Pillory". The calculating Harley, having decided that Defoe's pen would be useful, waited several months to insure Defoe's gratitude and then arranged his release from prison. Defoe was now a hero to the London mob and was secretly bound to the ambitious Harley.

SECRET AGENT DEFOE

Robert Harley (later created Earl of Oxford) became Secretary of State in 1704. He was a moderate Tory, but Defoe seemed to have no trouble in adapting his political beliefs to conform with Harley's. There was, basically, little difference between the moderate Whig and Tory positions. Defoe's duties, as Harley's protege, consisted of writing pamphlets and newspaper articles in support of government policy, taking informal public opinion polls throughout England and "campaigning" for the election of Harley's supporters. His usefulness could last only as long as his connection with Harley remained a secret. Defoe remained a servant of the Ministry, through several different administrations, until the death of Queen Anne in 1714.

EDITOR AND JOURNALIST

While Defoe was travelling around England and Scotland on Harley's behalf, he was also occupied by his duties as editor of *A Weekly Review of the Affairs of France*. The name soon proved undescriptive of the contents, for in the *Review* (which came out thrice weekly) Defoe discussed a variety of timely subjects. (The *Review* and a number of publications like it were the eighteenth-century equivalent of *Time* and *Newsweek* although they gave more space to editorials than to actual news.) At the same time he published numerous pamphlets` and treatises giving his views on such things as economics, public morality and the great storm of 1703. Defoe's account of the great storm represents the beginning of his career as a reporter. He investigated the effects of the storm himself, and secured descriptions of it from many people who witnessed it. He also reported on such strange matters as the alleged disappearance of an island in the West Indies and a ghostly visitation which he called The Apparition of Mrs. Veal.

UNOFFICIAL GOVERNMENT CENSOR

After Queen Anne's death in 1714, Defoe was without government employment for a time until George I's Whig Cabinet decided to make use of his talents. By this time, Defoe's association with the moderate Tory Harley was well known, and it was thought that Defoe was himself a Tory. It was therefore easy for him to obtain a position as editor of a Tory newspaper. What was not known was that he was in the employ of the Whigs and that his purpose was to soften the Tory attacks on the Government. Defoe's principal association was with the *Weekly Journal* published by Nathaniel Mist. Defoe served as an unofficial government censor on extreme Tory periodicals for several years, acting so circumspectly that no one suspected his connection with the Whig ministry.

FAMILY LIFE

Defoe's marriage to Mary Tuffley appears to have been reasonably happy. They had two sons and six daughters, but two of the daughters died young. Some biographers have asserted that Defoe also had an illegitimate son, but John Robert Moore, in his biography, *Daniel Defoe: Citizen of the Modern World*, denies this, One of Defoe's sons, Benjamin, became a journalist, but lacked his father's ability. Defoe's youngest daughter, Sophia, was his favorite. There are hints in Defoe's letters and moralistic treatises that his sons, particularly Daniel, Jr., were ungrateful and lacking in respect for their father.

ECONOMIST

Defoe was extremely interested in economics. *The Review* devoted more space to this subject than to any other. One of his most popular works was *The Complete English Tradesman* (1725) in which he gave sound advice, most of it based on his own business failures. His first book, *Essay on Projects* (1698) contained many excellent suggestions for improving the English economy, such as an income tax, more lenient treatment of bankrupts and improvements in the banking system.

ROBINSON CRUSOE

By 1719, Defoe's political career was coming to an end. However, in the remaining twelve years of his life, Defoe published a great many works, including all of his novels, several historical and biographical works and his famous *A Tour thro' the whole Island of Great Britain*. It is remarkable that the bulk of his literary compositions was written when he was past fifty. *Robinson*

Crusoe, published in 1719, was immensely popular during his lifetime. It was based on the adventures of a man named Alexander Selkirk, who lived alone for four years on an island, and purported to be autobiographical, rather than fictional. *Robinson Crusoe* was so successful that Defoe brought out two further volumes, *Further Adventures of Robinson Crusoe*, and *Serious Reflections of Robinson Crusoe*, neither of which is much remembered today.

MOLL FLANDERS: BACKGROUND

A popular literary form at this was time the criminal life, or rogue biography. Condemned criminals would give their stories to someone for publication. Enterprising journalist, among them Defoe, frequently paid the condemned man to hand them the manuscript (previously written by the journalists himself) at the gallows, thus gaining considerable free publicity. Since the lives of most of these unfortunates were not terribly interesting, most of the biographies contained more fiction than fact. *Moll Flanders* was written in this tradition and, like *Robinson Crusoe*, was supposed to be the autobiography of a real person. Although the novel is supposed to have been written in 1683, Defoe published it (and probably wrote it) in 1722. In *Moll Flanders*, Defoe describes England, and especially London, as it was in the early eighteenth century.

MOLL FLANDERS: PLOT

The full title of *Moll Flanders* gives an excellent description of the contents: "The Fortunes and Misfortunes of the Famous Moll Flanders, who was born in Newgate, and during a Life of continued Variety, for Threescore Years, besides her Childhood, was Twelve Year a Whore, five times a Wife (whereof once to her own Brother), Twelve Year a Thief, Eight Year a Transported Felon in Virginia, at last grew Rich, lived Honest, and died a Penitent, Written from her own Memorandums ..." The title is obviously designed to attract those who want to mix sensational reading with moral uplift. Moll's mother, convicted of stealing a small amount of cloth, was saved from the gallows only because of her pregnancy. By strange turns of fortune, Moll spends her 'teens with a moderately wealthy family. She becomes the mistress of the elder brother and then marries the younger brother. When her husband dies she marries a spendthrift and when he flees the country to avoid debtor's prison, marries once more, this time to a wealthy American. To her dismay, she finds after several years that her American husband is also her half-brother. Returning to England, Moll becomes mistress to a married man. When he leaves her, Moll marries for the fourth time. Her new husband, Jemmy, soon reveals that he is penniless and that he has married her only because he thought she was wealthy. They part affectionately agreeing that each is free to remarry. Moll soon marries for the fifth time and when, after some years, she is left a widow, she enters on a life of crime. Nearly half the book recounts Moll's profitable, though illegal career, but finally she is caught, taken to Newgate prison and sentenced to death. Her plea that her sentence be commuted to transportation to the colonies is granted and, having discovered that Jemmy is awaiting trial as a highwayman, she convinces him to go with her. Arriving in Virginia, Moll and Jemmy buy their freedom and begin a new life as planters. The novel ends with Moll's declaration that she and Jemmy, who are now elderly and wealthy, intend to spend the remainder of their lives in sincere repentance.

MOLL FLANDERS: PURPOSE

Defoe makes it quite clear, in his preface to *Moll Flanders*, that there is a moral to the story. Molls "fortunes and misfortunes" illustrate the maxim that "crime does not pay." Throughout the novel, Moll reprimands herself for her evil life and laments that her poverty compels her to embrace a life of crime. Defoe also manages to insert several of his schemes for the prevention of crime. For instance, he has Moll suggest that the government care for the children of criminals, training them to be useful individuals. While, toward the end of her life, Moll repents of the evil she has done, we note that she does not do so until she is financially secure and quite elderly. Some critics maintain that Defoe merely inserted moral comments to justify an otherwise sensational story. However, difficult though it is to believe, it appears that Defoe really thought that the lurid details of *Moll Flanders* would serve as a warning and encourage readers to amend their lives.

DEFOE'S OTHER NOVELS

Most of Defoe's novels are of the same **genre** as *Moll Flanders*, the rogue biography. *Colonel Jack*, which appeared toward the end of 1722, involved the hero in both crime and political rebellion. However, Colonel Jack repents (before old age sets in), becoming a highly respectable gentleman. The story of another rebel is recounted in *The Memoirs of a Cavalier* (1720). In the same year appeared *Captain Singleton*, which combines the current interest in far-off places (half the book is set in Madagascar) with the rogue biography. Another of Defoe's more famous novels is *Roxana*, published in 1724. Roxana is a lady of pleasure who seems to have no moral sense at all. However, in the end she too repents. All of Defoe's novels, including *Robinson*

Crusoe, have highly righteous endings, This was due partly to Defoe's own religious training and to the prevailing temper of the times: it did not matter what the character did, so long as he was sorry afterwards.

DEFOE'S LAST YEARS

During most of his life, Defoe lived in the fear of debtors' prison. Although he had paid most of his debts by 1702, he knew that a creditor could demand full payment at any time. Defoe's political enemies sometimes arranged to have debts which had already been paid, or which had never been contracted, brought up for payment. In those days, there was little legal protection for a former bankrupt. During much of his career, Defoe had powerful friends who could keep him out of prison, but toward the end of his life he had no such protection. He took the precaution of transferring all of his property to his son Daniel, so that creditors would be unable to lay claims to it. In the last year of his life, Defoe went into hiding, probably to escape one of these creditors. He was so afraid of being found that he would not permit his family to visit him openly. Finally, on April 24, 1731, he died "of a lethargy" (probably meaning old age). After such a long and vigorous life, it seems anti-climactic that he should die, alone, and in furnished rooms. Two days later he was buried in obscurity, but even those journals politically opposed to him honored him in their obituaries.

INTRODUCTION TO ROBINSON CRUSOE

This adventurous novel is related in the first person by Robinson Crusoe, an English mariner. There are two general divisions in the book. In the first brief section, Crusoe describes his family and career up to the time he is shipwrecked on a remote island. The second part of the novel, which forms the bulk of the work, consists of a journal, or diary-like account of his experiences during his life on the island.

Defoe never used Chapter divisions, and thus lacked an easy mechanical aid in emphasizing dramatic moments as well as preparation for and punctuation for minor climaxes.

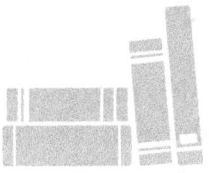

ROBINSON CRUSOE

TEXTUAL ANALYSIS

CHAPTERS 1 - 4

CHAPTER ONE

The narrator, Robinson Crusoe, was born in the year 1632, the third son of a German immigrant named Kreutznaer, who had settled in Hull, England. Being the third son, Robinson Crusoe (the name Kreutznaer was mispronounced by Englishmen) is not the prime interest in the family, and early in life, his thoughts turn from consideration of a middle-class trade to a life on the high seas. His father, a grave and temperate man, tells his son that the middle-station (middle-class) life is the best, and forbids him to seek a sea career, reminding the youth that the life of a sailor is one of desperate chances. Crusoe's older brother, a soldier, is killed in action, but his death does not keep Robinson from dreaming of going to sea. Finally, he agrees to accept an invitation, from one of his friends, to go to London by a ship which is owned by the latter's father.

No sooner does the ship sail down the Humber river to the sea when, suddenly, a storm breaks. Terrified by the crashing waves and wind, Crusoe fears for his life, viewing his suffering as a judgment by God for disobeying his father. He is determined to repent and return home when the storm is over. But once the storm abates, Crusoe joins his companions, drinks excessively of the sailors' punch, and soon forgets his fear-and his promise to himself.

CHAPTER TWO

After six days, the ship reaches Yarmouth Roads, where it lays at anchor for a week before continuing its voyage. On the next part of the voyage another and more violent storm occurs. Crusoe sees "terror and amazement" on the faces of the crew. The captain cries out, "Lord, be merciful to us! We shall all be lost; we shall be all undone!" In the middle of the storm the ship springs a leak; all hands begin to bail out the four feet of water in the hold. The ship begins to fire distress signals; luckily, another smaller ship appears and sends a small boat to enable the crew to escape.

CHAPTER THREE

After landing safely in the port of Winterton-Ness, Crusoe and the crew make their way on foot to Yarmouth and are given money to return home by the magistrates of the town.

Unwilling to return home to face the embarrassing comments of his father and friends about his sea career, Crusoe travels to London and soon agrees to take another ship-a ship bound for the coast of Africa. The friendly captain of the ship advises Crusoe to buy items in London to sell in Africa. On the voyage he studies navigation and mathematics, returning both as a "sailor" and a "merchant." The forty pounds of goods he sells enables him to reap a total of three hundred pounds. Although his friend, the captain, has died in Crusoe's absence, he is determined to repeat the profitable voyage. Taking command of a second ship, he leaves two hundred pounds in charge of the captain's widow.

Comment

Early in the novel we perceive two values of the author, which will influence his treatment of the entire work: 1) Defoe admired the middle-class level of society. Implicit in Defoe's *Robinson Crusoe* is an identification of family, social and divine order, all of which are flouted by Crusoe's deeds. Since human affairs are governed by Providence, any attempt to alter the established pattern implies a denial of God's power. The extraordinary interest which Providence takes in the "middle station" is illustrated by Crusoe's father extolling the upper station of low life as the best in the world and the most suited to human happiness. He prays "give me neither poverty nor riches; feed me with food convenient to me: Lest I be full, and deny thee, and say who is the Lord? or lest I be poor, and steal, and take the name of my God in vain." 2) God's providence shapes the lives of men. Defoe was an ardent believer in God, and thought that unusual circumstances of fortune and chance concealed a heavenly purpose. We see how Crusoe interprets the storm as a punishment for his refusal to listen to his father's admonition. Throughout the novel we will observe other instances of divine intervention in Crusoe's life.

CHAPTER FOUR

On the second African voyage, Crusoe's ship is suddenly attacked by Turkish pirates and the crew is captured. The prisoners are brought to the port of Sallee, (which then belonged to the Moors) where Crusoe is forced to become the slave of the pirate captain. When the captain goes to sea he leaves Crusoe on shore to look after his little garden and to perform the common drudgery of the slaves around his house.

But Crusoe's thoughts are always of escape. Whenever his Moorish master goes fishing he takes Crusoe and Xury, a young slave boy, with him. One day, unable to go fishing because of business, the Moor sends Crusoe, the boy, and another man out in the longboat, which he had taken from the ship, to catch fish for supper.

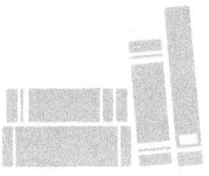

ROBINSON CRUSOE

TEXTUAL ANALYSIS

CHAPTERS 5 - 9

CHAPTER FIVE

Crusoe sees his chance for escape. He tells the man, Moley, to fetch provisions, water, and some powder and shot to take aboard the boat. After the three have been fishing for a while, Crusoe makes his move. He takes the Moor by surprise and throws him overboard. The man swims to shore. Crusoe turns to the young boy and offers his a choice: "Xury, if you will be faithful to me I will make you a great man; but if you will not stroke your face to be true to me" (that is, swear by Mohomet and his father's beard), "I must throw you into the sea too." The boy agrees to serve Crusoe and they make good their escape. They sail for five days before heading inland to a river along the coast.

They drop anchor for the night. In the morning a group of savages comes down to the beach to wash. Crusoe and Xury see one of the men swimming out to their boat. Taking up his gun,

Crusoe fires, frightening the swimmer back to shore. The pair quickly sail away, proceeding down the coast. Because their water supply is almost gone, they find it necessary to anchor several times and to wade ashore looking for water. On one island they catch and eat the flesh of an animal resembling a boar. Crusoe's main hope is to meet a European ship, and on one island, they wait for ten days peering for sails on the horizon. He and Xury become friendly with the natives, shoot a leopard for them and receive roots, corn and water in exchange.

Comment

Crusoe's continuing misfortune now results in his capture by the Turkish pirates. Yet Defoe shows us how resourceful an Englishman can be, by having Crusoe devise a clever and daring escape. Crusoe's resourcefulness is also an indication of a character trait-his very practical nature. This ties in with Defoe's own background. He was very religious, but was very practical when he dealt with the present everyday occurrences, or when the unexpected happened.

CHAPTER SIX

"Master, master, a ship with a sail!" cries Xury. It is a Portuguese ship, one probably bound for Africa, thinks Crusoe. He waves a flag, then fires a shot, as signals of distress. In three hours he and Xury are safely aboard the ship. A Scottish sailor on board translates Crusoe's story to the Portuguese captain, who treats him with great charity. After a twenty-two day voyage, the ship lands in the Bay de Todos los Santos (All Saints Bay), in Brazil. The captain buys Crusoe's longboat for eighty pieces of eight

(Spanish coin worth about one dollar), and even buys Xury from Crusoe for sixty pieces of eight. He wishes to use him as a servant.

CHAPTER SEVEN

In Brazil, Crusoe sells his guns and skins, and finds that he now has a fairly large sum of money. He becomes acquainted with a man who owns a sugar cane plantation and soon learns how to plant, raise and produce sugar. He buys some land, and, after three years, enlarges his crop to include tobacco. Crusoe sends word to England to the captain's widow, who sends him a great store of valuable manufacturers, bought with money he had left with her. Crusoe now begins to prosper. Living for four years on the plantation, however, is not very adventurous and Crusoe is ready for new experiences.

CHAPTER EIGHT

Crusoe agrees to a business venture with several Spanish planters, one in which they secretly fit out a ship to go to Guinea to bring back Negroes to work on their plantations. Crusoe is to go on the ship to manage the trading on the Guinea coast.

Yet he has misgivings. Why should he leave his plantation to venture on a risky voyage? Crusoe makes a will, leaving his estate to the Portuguese captain who saved him. One half of his wealth is to be kept by the captain, the other half is to be sent to England. Although he knows it is unwise he is resolved to go on the voyage-"I was hurried on, and obeyed blindly the dictates of my fancy, rather than my reason."

Comment

Once more God has seen fit to rescue Crusoe. We can see that practical nature of his pay off-the money he left in the widow's care, and which he sent for when he reached Brazil, is now helping him to start a new life. But, as Crusoe grows tired of the plantation life, he resolves to go searching for Negroes on the Guinea coast, thus looking for new adventure, and, also, emphasizing Defoe's belief that man is sinful and never satisfied with a simple, virtuous life.

Notice Defoe's method of telling the story: in pattern, he uses the narrative, fictional autobiography, pretending that it is "true," by using clever detail which sounds very authentic.

CHAPTER NINE

On the first of September, 1659, eight years after having left his parents' home at Hull in an act of rebellion to authority, Crusoe's ship sets sail. After twelve days at sea, a violent tornado strikes; it buffets the ship for twelve days before abating. Consulting his charts, Crusoe thinks it wise to sail towards the Barbados Islands to gain relief for the ship and crew. He changes the course of the ship, but soon a second storm descends, driving the ship far out of the usual sea lanes. Finally, one morning, one of the crew cries, "Land!" The crew runs to the side of the ship-suddenly, there is a jarring thud: the ship has run aground on a sand bar!

Expecting the ship to crack under the heavy wind, the crew decides to abandon ship and to risk sailing to the strange island. Crusoe and a few other men board a boat and begin the perilous journey to shore. Fearful that they will all be dashed to pieces on the shore, the men begin to pray as they row. A huge, raging wave suddenly swallows up the boat, scattering its occupants into the water. Wave after wave crashes over the heads of the unfortunate victims. Crusoe, half-dead with the water he has swallowed and with struggling in the waves, is carried towards the shore. Touching the ground with his feet, he begins to run to escape the next wave's charge, but twice more he is lifted by the waves and carried further in towards shore. Finally, he is thrown against a large rock, which he clings to, although he is left almost senseless from the blow. He waits to regain his strength, then makes a run for the shore. Clambering up onto a grassy bank, he sits-at last he is safe from the sea.

Comment

Defoe assessed the temperament of youth as follows: "Folly that is bound up in the Heart of a Child, says Solomon, is driven by the Rod of Correction ... What this folly is, needs no Description here, other than allow'd Custom in doing Evil, a natural Propensity we all have to Evil; with this we are born into the World, the Soul is originally bent to Folly."

A great portion of Defoe's philosophy is based on the concept of original sin, which is inherent in the concept of Divine Providence. For being a creature of sinful ways, Crusoe is feeling the lash of God's anger when he finds himself stranded on this unknown island.

ROBINSON CRUSOE

TEXTUAL ANALYSIS

CHAPTERS 10 - 18

CHAPTER TEN

Crusoe thanks God for his deliverance. He walks about making a thousand gestures and motions, reflecting upon his drowned comrades. How far off at sea is the ship? How did he ever manage to get ashore? With night coming on, Crusoe, fearful of ravenous beasts, seeks out and sleeps in a thick, bushy tree. The next morning he is surprised to find the ship lifted off the sandbar and much closer to land. Since it is a calm, bright day, Crusoe decides to swim out to the ship to see if anything of value may be salvaged. With great difficulty, he lifts himself aboard with the aid of a rope which was hanging over the side of the ship.

The ship is full of water, but Crusoe finds the food stores dry. He fills his pockets with biscuits to eat as he begins to explore the rest of the ship. He finds some rum, a drink of which buoys his spirits. His chief concern is to find a boat to use to carry the things he needs to shore. Ingeniously, Crusoe makes a light raft from seven extra sails. He uses the ship carpenter's tools to cut a spare mast into three sections. He next loads the makeshift raft with provisions and equipment: bread, rice, three Dutch cheeses, five pieces of goat's flesh, corn, the carpenter's chest of tools, ammunition, two guns and two rusty swords.

CHAPTER ELEVEN

Crusoe sails his raft along the beach for a mile, turning inland to the mouth of a little river. He spies a cove (a small bay or inlet) on the right shore, where he safely lands with his cargo.

Seeking a place to stow his goods, he ascends a steep hill a mile from the beach. He discovers that he is on an island totally surrounded by the sea. No land can be seen except for some rocks a great way off and two small islands to the west. The island is uninhabited and barren. Crusoe shoots large fowl but finds its flesh unfit to eat. Returning to the river bank, Crusoe spends the rest of the day removing his cargo. That night, he constructs a rude hut out of canvas and sea chests, then falls asleep.

CHAPTER TWELVE

The next morning, after making a second raft, he returns to the ship to obtain further provisions-bags of nails, spikes, a screw-jack, hatchets, a grindstone, iron crows, two barrels of musket bullets, seven muskets, gun shot, bedding, a roll of sheet lead, and clothing.

In the next eleven days, Crusoe returns to the ship ten more times, each time salvaging something useful to him. He takes all the rigging, rope and twine-even the sails of the ship. He finds a hogshead (a large cask) of bread, three large rum runlets (a barrel having the capacity of about eighteen gallons), a box of sugar and a barrel of fine flour.

On his last trip, Crusoe finds a few knives and forks; he then spies some English money-gold and silver coins. He exclaims "O Drug! What art thou good for? Thou art not worth to me, no, not the taking off the ground; one of those knives is worth all this heap; I have no manner of use for thee; e'en remain where thou art, and go to the bottom, as a creature whose life is not worth saving." Upon second thought Crusoe decides to take the money. That night a storm arises; and next morning the ship is no more to be seen.

Comment

We see how quickly Crusoe responds to the challenge of his situation. He does not hesitate to view his predicament in a practical light, immediately deciding to swim to the ship to save what he can from it. Defoe likes to describe in detail the various goods which his character finds.

Crusoe's speech about the usefulness of money is one of the most famous passages in the book. It is interesting to note, however, that in the next line he has a sudden change of heart, deciding to keep the money after all. Defoe's keen awareness of the real value of money in his business careers may have prompted him to have his hero save it.

One can see a pattern of an idea forming in the story: When man goes against God, he is always punished. So far, Crusoe has been severely punished for sinning. On his first voyage, when he disobeyed his father, he was in a storm; for pursuing the sea as a career, he was captured by Turkish pirates; for "slaving," he is cast upon an island, his ship wrecked upon the beach. The concept of "Divine Providence" is very apparent throughout the book.

CHAPTER THIRTEEN

Crusoe's thoughts now turn to providing himself a better dwelling to protect him from wild beasts or savages-should any appear. He finds a plain on the side of a rising hill, whose front is as "steep as a house-side" so that nothing can come down on him from the top. On the side of the rock is a hollow place (not really a cave but like the door of a cave). On the flat of this green, Crusoe pitches his tent. The plain is almost a hundred yards wide and two hundred yards long. He pitches high sharp spikes around his tent to make a strong fence or barricade, using a short ladder to gain access to the "house." He pulls the ladder over the fence with him when he enters, thereby leaving himself completely fortified. To protect his goods, he makes a small tent, covering it with a larger tent, over which he spreads a tarpaulin to protect his store from the rain. He then digs out much of the dirt in the cave-like hole in the rock to use it as a cellar.

CHAPTER FOURTEEN

Frightened by the thoughts of the possibility of lightning igniting his powder, Crusoe spends two weeks making over a hundred small parcels of powder which he hides in his cellar and in holes in the rocks.

Each day he goes hunting for food. He kills goats (of which there are many) by going up into the rocks and shooting down on them. Crusoe's reason for doing this is clever:

"I concluded, that by the position of their optics, their sight was so directed downward, that they did not readily see objects that were above them: so afterwards, I took this method-I always climbed the rocks first, to get above them, and then had frequently a fair mark."

CHAPTER FIFTEEN

The stranded Crusoe now begins to think about his state and condition. Sometimes the tears roll down his face when he considers that he is forsaken on a desolate island. Then he reconsiders: Did not eleven men go into the boat? Where are the other ten? Why were they not saved? It also occurs to him that he was indeed fortunate to have salvaged so much from the ship. What would he have done without a gun, without ammunition, without tools to make anything? His final conclusion is that "All evils are to be considered with the good that is in them, and with what worse attends them."

Comment

Again we see the practical philosophy of Defoe in Crusoe's positive attitude about his situation, one in which many men might have despaired. Crusoe is a very independent and resourceful individual, as is shown by his methods of securing himself a dwelling place. He thinks a project through to the very end. The logic he uses is very efficient when hunting goats, so as not to frighten them away. He thinks and provides himself with the necessities for future use-he is a long-range thinker.

CHAPTER SIXTEEN

To prevent losing track of time and particularly of the Sabbath, Crusoe constructs a post, carving into it the following sentence. "I came on shore here on the 30th of September, 1659." Upon the sides of this post he cuts a notch every day, the longer notches showing the seventh day of the week and the first of each month.

To deliver his mind from despondent thinking on his condition, Crusoe makes a list of his comforts and miseries:

Evil

I am cast upon a horrible, desolate island, void of all hope of recovery.

I am singled out and separated, as it were, from all the world, to be miserable.

I am divided from mankind, a solitaire; one banished from human society.

I have no clothes to cover me.

I am without any defence, or means to resist any violence or beast.

I have no soul to speak to, or relieve me.

Good

But I am alive; and not drowned, as all my ship's company were.

But I am singled out too from all the ship's crew, to be spared from death; and He that miraculously saved me from death, can deliver me from this condition.

But I am not starved, and perishing in a barren place, affording no sustenance.

But I am in a hot climate, where, if I had clothes, I could hardly wear them.

But I am cast on an island where I see no wild beasts to hurt me, as I saw on the coast of Africa: and what if I had been shipwrecked there?

But God wonderfully sent the ship in near enough to the shore, that I have got out so many necessary things, as will either supply my wants, or enable me to supply myself, even as long as I live.

CHAPTER SEVENTEEN

Having decided, then, that no condition in the world is so bad that some good cannot be found in it by which one may find something to comfort himself, Crusoe decides to enlarge his cave, making entrances and exits at two points in the cave and making more room for his supplies. He next makes himself a table and chair from the short pieces of boards he has brought from the ship. Because he has few tools, he is forced to make any boards he needs by cutting down a tree, and hewing laboriously until it becomes flat on both sides. He can, therefore, make only one board from an entire tree. Having had no previous experience working with tools, he finds, after diligent work, that "I wanted nothing but I could have made it, especially if I had had tools...."

Comment

Crusoe methodically keeps a calendar, so he can tell how long he remains on the island. Crusoe's list of the "good" and "evil" aspects of being stranded on the island shows that he is resigned to the fact that his predicament is the will of God, and that he must try to be happy if it is to be his plight.

CHAPTER EIGHTEEN

Crusoe now begins to keep a journal of his experiences, explaining that he would have done so sooner had not he been in "discomposure" of mind, and might have recorded "dull" things such as his escape from the ship.

Sept. 30, 1659: "I poor miserable Robinson Crusoe, being shipwrecked, during a dreadful storm, in the offing, came on shore on this dismal unfortunate island, which I called the Island of Despair; all the rest of the ship's company being drowned and myself almost dead."

Comment

This chapter marks the major division in the novel, for now Defoe has Crusoe relate, in diary form, his experiences on the island from the first day. Much of what Defoe has already told us is recounted in the early part of the journal; for example, he summarizes his numerous trips to the wrecked ship, his killing of the wild goats for food, and his excavation of the cave. Crusoe records incidents in the beginning of the journal which are not told to the reader earlier in the book; these dates and incidents I have mentioned above.

Defoe emphasizes the loneliness of being separated from civilization by Crusoe's calendar and the journal, which he keeps. Neither one is taken for granted, and both are very important in the daily life of our hero. Both the calendar and the journal are civilized concepts and emphasize the lack of civilized amenities in Crusoe's existence.

One senses that Defoe may be striving for ironic humor in the last remark of Crusoe's. One of the chief complaints by certain critics is that *Robinson Crusoe* lacks humor. To have the hero of the novel apologize for failing to write of a harrowing experience for fear of boring the reader may be an attempt by Defoe to show how excessively serious Crusoe is.

Nov. 5: Hunting with a dog he has saved from the ship, Crusoe sees several seals at the sea's edge.

Nov. 18: Lacking a wheelbarrow in which to carry things, he makes a hod (a wooden device used by bricklayers to carry mortar).

Nov. 23: He thatches his "house" with large leaves.

Dec. 17: From this day to the 20th he makes shelves for his house.

Dec. 24: "Much rain all day and night; no stirring out."

Dec. 25: "Rain all day."

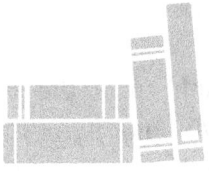

ROBINSON CRUSOE

TEXTUAL ANALYSIS

CHAPTERS 19 - 38

CHAPTER NINETEEN

From January 3rd to April 14, Crusoe tells us, that he spent his time finishing a wall around his house. When the wall is finished, and the outside area is double-fenced, Crusoe feels secure, and that if any people were to come on shore they would not perceive anything like a habitation. Then he adds, "and it was very well I did so, as may be observed hereafter, upon a very remarkable occasion."

Crusoe finds young pigeons in their tree nests, brings them to his cave, and begins to breed them. When they mature, however, they fly away. He decides, therefore, to eat the young pigeons when he finds them, since their meat is good.

In managing his household affairs, Crusoe finds he lacks many things - items which he cannot make himself. One of the items Crusoe tries to make without success is a cask. He tries many times but is unable to fit the staves together so as to make them hold water. Another item which he needs is candles. Because it is dark, he is forced to go to bed each night at seven o'clock. His only remedy is to save the tallow from the young goats he kills. With a little dish of clay baked in the sun and a small homemade wick of oakum (hemp fiber got by taking apart old ropes) Crusoe fashions a lamp. It works, but it does not give the clear, steady light of a candle. Crusoe also conceives an idea whereby he can turn a grindstone and sharpen his tools at the same time.

Comment

Defoe permits Crusoe to make the remark "and it is very well I did so as may be observed hereafter, upon a very remarkable occasion," at this point in the novel to whet our curiosity. One of the delights in a literary work is to know early that something is going to occur and later to learn what it is.

CHAPTER TWENTY

One day, while rummaging through his things, Crusoe discovers a bag of seed, partially eaten by the rats aboard ship. Throwing the remaining corn-like seeds away, he is startled to discover some weeks later that several stalks of English barley are growing near his house. Crusoe at first thinks the sprouts are miraculous growth put there by God. Later, when he remembers throwing away the seed, he still considers God's providence responsible. Because he had thrown it in the shade of a high rock, it sprang up immediately; whereas, "if I had thrown it anywhere else, at that time, it would have been burned up and destroyed."

Crusoe carefully saves all of his first crop, resolving to sow a crop each year. But it is not until his fourth year that he permits himself to eat anything of his crop, because he loses much of his first crop by failing to sow in the proper season.

Comment

Crusoe mentions the "fourth year," suggesting that his solitary stay on the island will also be a long one. One of the remarkable aspects of Defoe's handling of the novel is his ability to sustain our interest simply by describing, in realistic fashion, the daily events and processes in Crusoe's life.

Part of the Divine Providence concept is that everything is received by the direction of God. Defoe may have considered a parable from the New Testament in which a sower goes out to sow his seed; some seed is thrown in the thorns or on the rocks and perishes; some is thrown in rich soil and flourishes.

CHAPTER TWENTY-ONE

By April 14th, having worked "excessively hard" for months to finish a wall around his house, Crusoe finally completes it. By April 16th he finishes his ladder. On April 17th some of the earth on the roof of his cave crumbles down, narrowly missing Crusoe. He leaves his cave to discover that an earthquake has struck the island. The ground shakes several times at intervals of eight minutes, with three great shakes. A great piece of the top of a rock a half mile from his house falls violently into the sea. A hurricane descends soon after the quake. In his terror, Crusoe cries out "Lord, have mercy upon me!" After three hours, it becomes calm, and then begins to rain very hard.

Crusoe cuts a hole in his fortification to let out the rain water-deciding he must move away from the cave to avoid further danger from earthquakes and storms.

CHAPTER TWENTY-TWO

On May 1st, he discovers a barrel of wet gunpowder on the beach. Washed ashore from the wreck of the ship, it is caked and "hard as a stone." The ship itself has been tossed toward shore. The months of May and June find Crusoe trekking back and forth to the ship retrieving, with much difficulty, iron work, planks and beams-enough to make a good boat, if he knew how. On June 16th and 17th, he finds, kills, cooks and eats a tortoise, the first flesh other than goats and fowls that he has eaten since landing "in this horrid place."

CHAPTER TWENTY-THREE

June 18th, a cold rainy day, finds Crusoe in the first stages of illness. His condition becomes gradually worse, and he suffers violent pains in his head, and has fits of extreme hot and cold. By June 27th, he is so weak, now, that he cannot stand up-he prays, "Lord, look upon me! Lord, pity me! Lord, have mercy upon me!" He then falls asleep and dreams that he sees a man descend from a great black cloud, in a bright flame of fire; as he alights upon the ground, the earth begins to quake; the air is filled with flashes of fire. He approaches Crusoe with a long spear in his hand, then roars in a terrible voice, "Seeing all these things have not brought thee to repentance, now thou shalt die."

Crusoe discusses the dream in light of his past indifference towards religion and his disobedience to his father's wishes.

Crusoe cries aloud, "Now, my dear father's words are come to pass: God's justice has overtaken me, and I have none to help or hear me ... Lord, be my help, for I am in great distress."

Comment

Here, Defoe injects what amounts to a sermon on the need for every man to lead a good life. Notice how accurately Defoe constructs Crusoe's dream in light of his experience on the island. Crusoe has been terrified by an earthquake and now, lying ill and fearing he will die, he dreams of a revenging Justice (God) coming to earth (the ground quakes on his arrival) to admonish him for his sins and his refusal to repent for them.

Crusoe remembers his father's thoughts on what the proper station in life is. He thinks that this is his just punishment for not heeding his father's advice.

CHAPTER TWENTY-FOUR

June 28: Crusoe's health has improved considerably by June 28th, and he makes some dinner of turtle eggs. Although still weak, he walks out to sit and look at the sea. He asks, "Why has God done this to me? What have I done to be thus used?" Crusoe answers himself that God is the source and guide of everything; therefore God has known and willed that Crusoe be spared from death-decreeing that he should live alone on the island as punishment for his past life.

After drinking a mixture of rum and tobacco (which was thought to have medicinal value by the Brazilians) Crusoe sleeps soundly-for what he thinks is two days and nights. Years later, in his reckoning of the time he has spent on the island, he loses one day and can account for it no other way than by judging that he slept through two days during his illness.

Crusoe finds a Bible among his goods and opens it to the words, "Call on me in the day of trouble, and I will deliver thee, and thou shalt glorify me." Crusoe wonders, then prays to God to be delivered, if some day he asks of his aid.

Comment

This scene, after the illness, displays more emotion than any other part of the book. It not only shows how strongly he felt about the influence of God's will in the affairs of men, but makes the futility of Crusoe's situation real to the reader. Before this **episode**, the reader is taken in by the story, not feeling much sympathy for Crusoe, because of his extreme ableness to care for his physical needs. Now, however, having gone through a serious illness, and needing the help of another human being, we sympathize for him. His cry to God, asking why to the question of his being forsaken, illustrates more than anything else his extreme loneliness and lack of human companionship.

CHAPTER TWENTY-FIVE

By July 3rd, the "fit" has left Crusoe for good-he is cured.

July 4: He reads in his Bible, "He is an exalted prince and a Savior; to give repentance and to give remission." Crusoe repents then cries out in joy; he says it is the first time in his life that he has truly prayed.

July 4th to July 14th, Crusoe is chiefly employed in walking about, and regaining his strength. He begins to explore the island, sailing down the creek to discover many rich plains full of green tobacco and other plants, which he does not recognize. He discovers rich clusters of grapevines, and he spends the night there, sleeping in a tree.

Crusoe's explorations take him four miles further along the island, where he discovers a fresh green country which looks "like a planted garden." Here there is an abundance of cocoa trees, orange, lemon, lime and citron trees (a yellow, thick-skinned fruit resembling a lime or lemon, but larger and contains less acid).

Crusoe thinks of moving his permanent residence to this fruitful vale, then reconsiders, wishing to remain as close as possible to the ocean, in hopes of someday seeing someone arrive on the island. He decides to build a bower or "summer house," as he calls it. Now he can say that he owns both a seacoast house and a country house.

From July 17th to August 3rd, Crusoe works on his new "country" house.

The month of August brings heavy, incessant rain. Crusoe finishes the inside of his "seacoast" house. The seasons of the year are divided not into summer and winter but into the rainy seasons and the dry seasons, which are, generally: from the middle of February to the middle of April, rainy; from the middle of April till the middle of August, dry; from the middle of August till the middle of October, rainy; form the middle of October to the middle of February, dry.

September 30th is the anniversary of his landing on the island. He keeps this day as a solemn fast setting it aside for religious exercise.

During the rainy season Crusoe makes wicker baskets from twigs. He wishes he had a small pot to make broth and stew, and a tobacco pipe to smoke.

CHAPTER TWENTY-SIX

Crusoe resolves to explore the whole island. He finds the other side of the island to be much pleasanter than his own. He notices hares and foxes, goats and pigeons. On the opposite seashore he sees innumerable turtles and even penguins. After walking twelve miles or so along the beach he marks an area with a post, deciding to return home and to travel someday in the other direction until he comes to the post again, thereby making a complete circle of the island. He rests for a week after his journey, admiring his new and affectionate friend-a parrot- which he has found in his recent travels.

September 30th, Crusoe's second anniversary, is observed in the same manner as the first.

Comment

Crusoe now skips time much faster than when he began the journal. Telling us that his ink supply is low (and since he cannot make more ink), he will record only those events of importance. Defoe, of course, wishes to give the reader a sense of the passing of time; therefore, many years will now be recorded in fewer pages than before.

CHAPTER TWENTY-SEVEN

Crusoe, now in his third year on the island, has changed his hierarchy of spiritual values. Whereas he cursed his position before, he now is beginning to exercise new thoughts; he reads the word of God daily, and takes great pleasure in rejoicing upon a passage in the Bible, where God says: "I will never, never leave thee, nor forsake thee." With this to believe, it is possible to be happy in the solitary life which he is confronted with.

His order of the day is the following: he reads the Bible three times a day; he spends three hours hunting for food; he cures, preserves and cooks what he has caught; and he spends the remainder of the day working. He is obliged to spend much time working on various projects because he has few tools. For instance, it takes forty-two days to make a board for a shelf. Fearful that wild goats will eat his crops, Crusoe builds a fence around them, but as the birds plague him, he shoots a few, and makes scarecrows of them, thus frightening away the other birds.

Comment

The reader can see the main character of the story become more and more reliant on God's salvation. This gives him the peace of mind to continue in a steadfast manner to live a normal life- as normal as possible under the circumstances. Defoe believed that the perfect life is man's acceptance of God, and his total reliance on the faith of God.

CHAPTER TWENTY-EIGHT

Crusoe describes his great efforts to sow and plant crops; how, for example, he is forced to drag a heavy bough of a tree over his land to "scratch" it, since he has neither a rake nor a plow. He also tells of his efforts to make a clay pot from his homemade paste: "It would make the reader laugh at me, to tell how many awkward ways I took to raise this paste, what odd, misshapen, ugly things I made; how many of them fell in, and how many fell out, the clay not being stiff enough to bear its own weight; how many cracked by the over-violent heat of the sun, being set out too hastily; and how many fell in pieces with only removing, as well before as after they were dried; and, in a word, how, after having laboured hard to find the clay, to dig it, to temper it, to bring it home, and work it, I could not make above two large earthen ugly things (I cannot call them jars) in about two months' labour." By luck, Crusoe is able to make a pot. One day, he finds broken pieces of his earthenware vessels in the fire, burned as hard "as stone and red as tile." He is agreeably surprised, judging that they might be made to burn whole, if they would burn broken. He, therefore, makes a huge fire and burns several pots. In the morning, after burning them, all night, he finally has his cooking pots.

Crusoe overcomes several difficulties in making utensils for bread-making. He makes a mortar out of a block of wood and a pestle from another piece of wood; now he can grind his corn crop to make bread. He makes sieves to sift husks out of his meal by punching holes in some old seamen's neckcloths saved from the ship. He makes his bread by putting it into a large earthenware pan, covering it with another pan, and placing the "oven" over red hot charcoal embers from his fire. He now learns to make cakes and puddings, but no pies, since he says he has nothing to put into them except the flesh of fowls or goats.

Comment

The scene where Crusoe is trying to make clay pots, none of which are finished satisfactorily, enables the reader to share vividly the frustration and success which he experienced. It is easy to identify with another human being who is learning a new skill by the usual trial-and-error process.

This last statement of Crusoe is in disagreement with what he has earlier told us: he has raisins, lemons, limes on the island and surely could use either (or all) of them as filling for pies. Defoe's inability to remain logical or consistent in this novel has prompted one critic to write an article in which he discusses instances in which Defoe forgets or changes information he has already given to the reader.

CHAPTER TWENTY-NINE

All the while he has been on the island, Crusoe has thought of finding a means of escape. He fells a cedar tree then spends three months clearing the inside with a mallet and chisel. But when he attempts to roll it to the ocean he finds it is too heavy for him to push it the hundred yards to the water. He thinks of cutting a canal to it, but judges such a project will take ten or twelve years.

Crusoe now finishes his fourth year on the island. He states of life as very comfortable: he has good food and shelter, tools for work, weapons for defense, and gunpowder and shot for getting his food. He often reflects back on how dreadful his life had been, saying that the life of a sailor is "destitute" of the knowledge of God.

His clothes are beginning to wear thin, and he must make new ones himself. First, he makes a great cap for his head and an umbrella for protection from the sun. He fashions both out of the skins of animals he has slain.

> Comment

Crusoe now is resigned to the fact that his present state is due to the will of God alone, and that God has been merciful and generous to him. He daily gives thanks for what he has-wanting "nothing to make it [his manner of living] a life of comfort, but to be able to make my sense of God's goodness to me, and care over me in this condition, be my daily consolation; and after I did make a just improvement of these things, I went away and was no more sad." Crusoe is relying more and more on an absolute faith in God's Word.

CHAPTER THIRTY

At this point in the journal, Crusoe tells us that nothing extraordinary happens to him for five more years. He then tells us of the desire he has during this period to go around the island in a boat. He builds a periagua (a small canoe), fitting it with a small sail, then fixing his umbrella at the stern, he embarks on a series of small cruises.

On the sixth day of November in his sixth year of his "reign of captivity," he sails to the east side of the island. He secures his boat and mounts a hill; from her he notices that a current of the water is so strong that it might carry his boat far out to sea. After two days, he ventures forth again when the is sea calm. Suddenly his boat, caught in the midst of two swift currents, begins to carry him away from the island. Crusoe cries out, "O happy Desert! I shall never see thee more: O miserable creature!"

Crusoe struggles to turn his ship back towards the island, but is unsuccessful until a current in the opposite direction and a change in the wind finally returns him safely to shore. He thanks God for his deliverance, and after having a meal, the exhausted Crusoe sleeps.

He resolves to sail west, back to his house, unwilling to risk further exploration. He first explores the region in which he has landed, eventually making his way to his "country house." Again he sleeps, but is awakened suddenly by a voice: "Robin, Robin, Robin Crusoe; poor Robin Crusoe! Where are you, Robin Crusoe? Where are you? Where have you been?" He awakens to find Poll, his parrot, staring at him! Overjoyed to again see the bird he has found and trained to speak, he carries him home, leaving his boat on the other side of the island.

Comment

Defoe interrupts his action here to observe that "we never see the true state of our condition till it is illustrated to us by its contraries, nor know how to value what we enjoy, but by the want of it." Poll Parrot's greeting vividly illustrates the fact the Crusoe is, indeed, very much alone in this world, and that for one to be happy in this life, one needs companionship.

CHAPTER THIRTY-ONE

Crusoe's journal now skips to his eleventh year on the island. The first part of this section of the journal describes Crusoe's success in raising a flock of goats. He traps them, in pits: then delivers them to a pen-eventually making five pastures, where they can graze. With over forty goats, he knows he has an available supply of flesh, milk, butter and cheese available at all times. In addition, he has barley, corn, raisins, grapes, citrus fruit. He sits at his table like a king, with Poll, his old dog, and two cats at his side. He has everything he could want-except the society of men-but soon he will have too much society.

Crusoe has refined his methods of manufacturing many of the necessities: he now can make his clay pots to appear more pleasing to the eye; and his clothing has become more sophisticated. He now makes his own smoking pipe, which overjoys him.

Crusoe now continues his narrative shortly after he begins another journey by land to the hill where he first saw the dangerous currents. He studies the flow of the waters and learns the flow and ebb of the tides so that he will easily be able to sail into the island when he attempts another voyage. Whenever he sails, he is apprehensive of being carried out to sea that he usually stays within a stone's throw of the island.

Comment

Defoe now hints of new adventures of Crusoe to whet our curiosity and to sustain our interest. Crusoe has established his economy on the island, and if the story were to continue in this vein, the reader would become bored. So, the author throws out hints of something new. Have you noticed that this is the second time that there has been a pause in the story? The first pause was when Crusoe started his journal. Defoe switched his method of telling the story. It may have been, according to some of his critics, that the author ran out of information, and was gathering his resources before starting up the story again. It is because of these pauses that Defoe lacks well-knit story structure.

CHAPTER THIRTY-TWO

One day, about noon, going towards his boat, Crusoe is startled to see the print of a man's naked foot in the shore! He stands thunderstruck. He listens, then looks around. Terrified, he runs to his house (his "castle" as he calls it), and spends a sleepless night thinking: how could anything human come to the island? Where was the ship that brought this man and perhaps others with him? He even believes that the Devil may have put the print in the sand to torment him, or that savages from the island near his may have been carried there by the currents.

Temporarily, Crusoe's fears overpower him to the point where he forgets the Divine Providence of God, and the possibility of closing a void which has existed for eleven years-conversation with another human being-is forgotten. The thing which he has yearned for is now dreaded with the utmost fear. Eventually, Crusoe thinks that he may have been imagining that he saw the footprint. After three days he returns to the beach. The print is indeed there. He sees that it is much larger than his own footprint. He returns home to make another wall as a fortification to his house and sits up at night to place his seven guns in holes to defend himself, if he must. He then plans how to protect his property-the goats and his grain.

CHAPTER THIRTY-THREE

For two years Crusoe lives in fear, constantly building his fortifications and preserving food. He makes new secret enclosures for his goats, to hide them as well. One day, while looking for another private place to deposit some goats, he thinks he sees a boat upon the sea at a great distance.

Coming down a hill at the end of the island, Crusoe thinks that it would not be unusual for natives to have frequently visited this part of this island, since his house was on the other side, and he would have no knowledge of their coming and going. Suddenly he perceives a horrible sight: the shore at the foot of the hill is strewn with skulls, hands, feet, and other bones of human bodies. "And, particularly, I observed a place where there had been a fire made, and a circle dug in the earth, like a cockpit, where I supposed the savage wretches had sat down to their inhuman feastings upon the bodies of their fellow-creatures."

Amazed and ill at the sight, Crusoe stumbles home to his castle. For two years he limits his actions to maintenance of his house and to his work. He is continually sad thinking of the inhumanity of what he has seen, but he is determined to keep himself concealed, fearful of the cannibal visitors.

CHAPTER THIRTY-FOUR

Eighteen years have passed since Crusoe's arrival. He is much more cautious in his travels than formerly, and is careful about firing his gun unnecessarily lest it attract attention. He carries two pistols and a huge cutlass for further protection. He gives up a pet project he had thought of beginning-the making of beer-to concentrate his efforts on a serious plan: "Night and day, I could think of nothing but how I might destroy some of these monsters in their cruel, bloody entertainment, and, if possible, save the victim they should bring hither to destroy."

Estimating that he will have to fight twenty or thirty natives, Crusoe imagines planting powder under their campfire sites to blow them up or of shooting three guns simultaneously when they are feasting, thereby killing or wounding most of them.

This latter plan pleases him more than the first. Accordingly, he loads several guns and makes continual expeditions to the top of the hill, to see if any cannibals have come. After several months of daily three-mile walks to the hill, Crusoe begins to ponder the justice involved in killing thirty men. Since the natives are barbarous, they do not have the same moral code as civilized men. He considers how ruthless the Spanish were in killing so many natives in their conquest of South America.

Comment

Defoe, a loyal Englishman, slashes an attack upon Spain, the enemy of his country. The practices of the Spanish forces in their settlement of Peru were bloody, and Defoe cannot resist stating his condemnation.

The passing of time helps Crusoe's reason to subdue his passion for revenge, and he resolves both in principle and policy not to meddle with natives. If one of them were to escape, he fears, he would return for revenge with thousands of his followers.

CHAPTER THIRTY-FIVE

Fear of discovery motivates Crusoe to put an end to all "invention and to all contrivances" which he had used for future comfort and convenience. All concern is focused on storing food and protecting himself. To escape discovery, Crusoe **refrains** from chopping wood or firing his gun. He builds charcoal fires in a cave to avoid making smoke.

One day, while exploring, he finds another small cave. The cave is very dry and high and can be entered only by crawling on one's hands and knees. Crusoe brings some of his gunpowder and arms and other supplies to his new retreat. Now, he thinks, he has an excellent hiding place to go if the need arises.

CHAPTER THIRTY-SIX

It is now December in the twenty-third year of his residence on the island. Going out early one morning, even before daylight, to harvest his fields, Crusoe is surprised to see a light on the shore, two miles away-on his side of the island! He returns to his castle, but after two anxious hours of waiting decides to go to the hill to explore. He sees nine savages, sitting around a fire; they have two canoes with them, hauled up on the shore. Crusoe concludes that they are waiting for the tide to change so they may return to their own island. He is correct, for an hour later when the tide is moving out, they leave. Going to the beach, Crusoe is shocked to find the marks of horror the savages have left behind: the blood, the bones, and other remnants of human bodies!

A year and three months pass. In the month of May of his twenty-fourth year, a great storm strikes the island. Crusoe stays inside his castle, reading his Bible. He is surprised to hear what sounds like the noise of a gun fired at sea. Hastily running to a hill, he hears a second shot-coming from that part of the island where he was driven by the current, in his boat.

He lights a fire and climbs to another hill. Using a spyglass, he views, to his great sorrow, the wreck of a ship, cast away on the distant rocks. A strong idea pervades Crusoe's mind: perhaps some men have been saved. But it is not to be. Some days later the corpse of a drowned boy is washed ashore near the wreck. In his pockets Crusoe finds two pieces of eight and an item he has always longed for in his solitude-a tobacco pipe.

CHAPTER THIRTY-SEVEN

Determined to explore the wrecked ship, Crusoe, after studying the currents of the water, sails out to the rocks. It is a Spanish ship. As he approaches, a dog leaps from the deck and swims to his boat. He feeds it some bread and water, then goes aboard the ship. In the galley he finds two dead men, their arms wrapped about each other. He takes several chests, a little cask of liquor, a powder horn, a fire shovel and tongs, two brass kettles, a copper pot, and a gridiron. With his cargo and the dog, he returns to the island. He opens the chests, which contain clothes and money. Both of these items are of little value, particularly the money: "I had no more use of it than the Indians of Peru had before the Spaniards came."

Two years pass. Crusoe seldom travels far from his side of the island. His chief thoughts during this time are concerned with ways of getting away from the island. His restlessness, he thinks, is natural; he calls it the "general plague" of mankind.

One night during the rainy season, in March of his twenty-fourth year, Crusoe has a curious dream: he sees two canoes and eleven savages. They have brought with them another savage whom they are going to kill, in order to eat him. Suddenly the prisoner jumps away and begins to run, hiding in the grove near Crusoe's fortification. Crusoe makes himself known to the man, who immediately makes motions to him for assistance. Bringing him to the safety of his cave, Crusoe teaches the savage to become his servant.

Upon waking, Crusoe at first is overjoyed by the dream. Soon, however, he becomes dejected, since it was, after all, only a dream. He is determined to capture a savage, and begins to plan in his imagination how he will accomplish such a plan.

Comment

Defoe's view, that one-half of the "miseries" of mankind may be traced to "not being satisfied with the station wherein God and nature have placed them," repeats a major **theme** of the novel and a chief tenet of eighteenth-century English thought. An intelligent person was one who recognized the folly of emotionally-directed acts-Crusoe's voyages. Man should learn to accept his place on the level in which he was born; he can thereby learn to be content with his life. Order and degree are needed by man-if he recognizes his place in life and accepts it, he will be reasonably happy-this is the middle-class mystique, which was discussed earlier.

CHAPTER THIRTY-EIGHT

One morning, about a year and a half after his dream, Crusoe is surprised to see five canoes on the shore on his side of the island. Climbing to the top of the hill, he perceives through his spyglass no less than thirty men. They have a fire kindled, and are dancing grotesquely around the fire. Two captive natives are dragged from the boats; one of them is clubbed and immediately murdered. The other, free momentarily, breaks from his captors and bounds quickly down the beach towards that part of the coast where Crusoe's habitation is situated.

At first, the escapee is pursued by three savages. He swims across a small river and only two follow, one being unable to swim. Deciding to help the man escape so as to gain himself a servant, Crusoe fetches his gun and steps in the way of the pursuers, motioning with his hand to the pursued man to return: "I slowly advanced upon the two that followed: then rushing at once upon the foremost, I knocked him down with the stock of my piece." Crusoe kills the other savage because he attempts to shoot an arrow at him. Upon beckoning to the man whose life he had saved, the native, advancing towards him, kneels every ten or twelve steps in token of acknowledgment for the saving of his life: "Then he kneeled down again, kissed the ground, and laid his head upon the ground, and taking me by the foot, set my foot upon his head: this, it seems, was in token of swearing to be my slave forever."

But there is yet work to do: the other savage is only stunned. The free man gestures to Crusoe for his sword. He swiftly kills the savage in a stroke, then buries both bodies. The two men return safely to Crusoe's cave.

In a little time, Crusoe begins to speak to his new servant, telling him that his name shall be "Friday," in memory of the day on which he had saved his life. He tells Friday to call him "Master." Friday is a "comely, handsome fellow, perfectly well-made with straight, strong limbs, not too large, tall, and well-shaped, and, as I reckon, about twenty-six years of age." He later tells Crusoe, by means of sign language, that there had been a great battle between the natives and he had been taken prisoner.

Crusoe gives him a pair of linen pants, a goatskin jacket, and a cap of hare's skin. At first he is suspicious of Friday and sleeps with all his weapons near him at night. But Crusoe needs no precautions, admitting, "Never man had a more faithful, loving, sincere servant than Friday was to me."

Comment

Defoe uses the device of a dream to signal subsequent events in the novel. Crusoe dreams of a savage escaping from his captors and becoming his servant; Friday is the reality he had dreamed about. This is a literary technique called "foreshadowing," in which the reader has the pleasure of watching a possibility in the novel becoming real, in the context of the novel.

Now, a new area is opened up for us-that of the education of Friday and the resultant companionship that it brings to Crusoe.

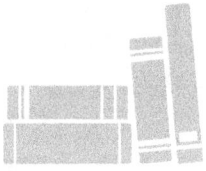

ROBINSON CRUSOE

TEXTUAL ANALYSIS

CHAPTERS 39 - 44

CHAPTER THIRTY-NINE

After two or three days, the men return to Crusoe's castle. Crusoe teaches Friday everything proper to make him useful and helpful, particularly how to speak. Friday is an apt scholar; he is also particularly merry as well as being constantly diligent. Crusoe explains to him the use of salt with meat and how to retrieve animals that he shoots. Friday thinks Crusoe's gun is a magical person; he speaks to it, and asks the gun not to shoot him.

Crusoe questions Friday about how he came to the island, asking about the savages:

Master: "Do they come hither?"

Friday: "Yes, yes, they come hither; come other else place."

Master: "Have you been with them?"

Friday: "Yes, I have been here."

By this method, Crusoe learns that the savages usually came to the other side of the island, but that a current and a wind caused by a great draft and reflex of the Oroonoko River (a fact Crusoe afterwards discovers) brought Friday and the other natives to his side of the island. Crusoe later discovers that the island to the northwest of his own is Trinidad. He finds that Friday is from the Caribees Islands, which reach from the mouth of the Oroonoko to Guiana. Crusoe estimates that they are relatively near South America, for even Friday has heard of the cruelties of the Spanish. Friday estimates that two men in a canoe could reach South America safely, a thought which excites Crusoe.

Crusoe begins to teach Friday the Christian religion. Friday says the Christian God must be greater than Benamuckee, the God of the Savages, who lives a little way off, but who cannot hear unless men go up to the mountains where he dwells to speak to him. Crusoe converts Friday and he becomes an exemplary Christian, so much so that Crusoe observes, "I have known few equal to him in my life."

Comment

The introduction of Friday is two-fold. Because of the religious element dominant throughout the book, Friday's appearance on the island allows Crusoe to impart the benefits of his own conversion to him.

Also, Crusoe's guidance of Friday displays the progress of Crusoe's faith and regeneration. This situation indicates the missionary zeal which was apparent among the dissenters of Defoe's time.

CHAPTER FORTY

It is now the twenty-seventh year of Crusoe's "captivity." Through their conversation, Crusoe learns from Friday that a Spanish or Portuguese ship had been wrecked off the coast of the island from which Friday comes, and the natives had rescued seventeen "bearded" men. They did not eat the white men, Friday explains, because cannibalism is only practiced during native civil war. Determined to go to the island, they seek out the old boat Crusoe had made twenty-three years earlier. Unable to use the rotted vessel, they fell a tree and together begin to build a new periagua or canoe. After several months of work, they have a boat with a mast and worn sails ready to launch.

One morning Friday comes rushing madly up from the seashore. "O yonder there," he says, "one, two, three canoe; one, two, three!" Crusoe resolves to fight and asks Friday to join him. Taking his spyglass, he ascends the hill, to discover twenty-one savages, three prisoners and three canoes on the beach.

In a fit of fury, Crusoe determines an attack. He and Friday equipped with guns and ammunition, make their way to within eighty yards of the savages. Concealed by bushes, they see two savages about to untie a white prisoner. Crusoe gives the signal to fire. Friday kills two men and wounds three; Crusoe kills one and wounds two. They fire again-killing and wounding more of the savages. Charging down to the beach, Crusoe frees the white man, a Spaniard, while Friday fires at three natives trying to escape in a canoe. The Spaniard picks up a sword and joins the fight. The battle is soon over; the losses of the natives are many-only four of the twenty-one escape-the remainder were all killed. Looking in one of the canoes, Crusoe finds another prisoner. Friday, looking at the old man, suddenly begins to jump and dance about, wringing his hands and shouting. He tells Crusoe that the man is his father.

Later, Crusoe learns from Friday's father that the natives who escaped probably have perished in the storm, which occurred that night, or if they do return safely to their own island, they will never return because they will think that the island is inhabited by spirits. He learns from the Spaniard that there are sixteen other Spaniards and Portuguese living peacefully on a nearby island. (This is the same one that Friday and his father are from.) They are the survivors of a Spanish ship bound from the Rio de la Plata to Havana.

Crusoe is determined to rescue the sixteen men; in six months he and the other three men build a boat. The Spaniard and Friday's father sail away to the island; all those who swear allegiance to Crusoe will be permitted to return with them to "Crusoe's" island.

Comment

We notice Defoe again employing the concept of fate to bring about a "surprise." Using the unexpected to startle the reader is one of his characteristics.

Defoe strangely fails to explain why and how Friday's father and the Spaniard became prisoners of the cannibals.

CHAPTER FORTY-ONE

Eight days pass. One morning Crusoe sees an English ship anchored out at sea, and a small boat making its way to land.

There are eleven men; three of them are bound prisoners. Crusoe sees the three men being beaten by the others. Following this action, five of the men begin to explore the island, leaving two men in a boat to watch the prisoners. The tide drifts out, and the boat becomes stuck on the sand. Returning to find the boat aground, the men who have been exploring the island resume their exploration, waiting for the tide to come in. One of the men says, "Why, let her alone, Jack, can't ye?"

Knowing the men will be ashore for at least ten more hours until the tide changes, Crusoe arms himself and Friday; seeing the three men unguarded, they walk boldly to the boat. Crusoe speaks to the men, volunteering aid. One of them tells him, "I was commander of that ship; my men have mutineered against me." Crusoe asks if their captors have firearms. He learns that the mutineers have two, but one is in the boat. There are two leaders of the mutiny, who have implored the others to join them. The captain tells Crusoe it is unnecessary to kill all of the crew. Crusoe makes the three men pledge to two conditions before he releases them: 1) While they stay on the island they will be ruled by him, surrendering to him any arms he may permit them to use. 2) If the ship is recovered, they will carry him and Friday to England, passage free.

Giving the men muskets, Crusoe watches as five of the mutineers return. The captain's two men fire, killing two of the bewildered sailors. All the mutineers are soon captured. Crusoe tells the captain of his experiences on the island, then suggests that the boat which brought in the mutineers be destroyed; accordingly, a great hole is knocked in its bottom. Soon another boat, containing ten men, comes from the ship. As they approach the land, the captain advises Crusoe that three or four of the men are "honest," that they would be loyal to him (Crusoe) if he gives them the chance. The men land, and begin to shout to their missing comrades; they also fire a volley of shots. Receiving no reply and fearing the worst, they begin to push off, then decide to have three men wait in the boat while the others explore.

Crusoe sends Friday and the captain's mate a half mile down the beach, telling them to shout as loud as they can. Upon hearing the shouts, the men begin to run towards Friday and the mate, leaving only two men in the boat. The captain and Crusoe overpower the pair, then wait for several hours for the others to return. Friday has led them through an exhausting journey; when they struggle back to the boat, the boatswain, the principal leader of the mutiny, and another man are killed by the captain and Friday. Crusoe and the others advance through the darkness to where the mutineers are assembled.

All the men surrender to Crusoe, who is now called the "governor." The captain says all men except Will Atkins, the man who had bound his hands and mistreated him during the mutiny shall be forgiven. Atkins immediately begs the captain for forgiveness.

Comment

Again our interest in quickened by the arrival of an English ship, which is anchored in the harbor. Now we see the possibility of Crusoe's escape drawing nearer, thus the action is quicker and more exciting.

CHAPTER FORTY-TWO

The chief design of Crusoe and the captain is to regain the ship. Accordingly, the first boat is repaired, and at midnight the two boats return to the ship. In the darkness one of the mutineers, Robinson, explains to the watch that it took a long time for the men in the second boat to find those who were in the first. The captain and his men surprise the crew, shoot the "new" captain and regain control of the ship. Seven guns are fired to notify Crusoe of the success of the plan.

Crusoe becomes speechless when he realizes the ship has been taken. Now he is free to leave the island! He writes, "Such was the flood of joy in my breast, that it put all my spirits into confusion; at last I broke out into tears; and in a little while after I recovered my speech."

Three of the worst mutineers are to be left on the island. Crusoe gives them food, muskets and powder and tells them how to manage the goats, make bread and cure grapes.

Wearing new clothes which the captain has given him, Crusoe takes his great goat skin cap, his umbrella and one of his parrots for souvenirs, then boards the ship. Thus he leaves the island on the 19th of December in the year 1686, after being there for twenty-seven years, two months and nineteen days; he is delivered from his "second" captivity on the same day of the month that he first made his escape in the longboat from the Moors of Sallee. After a long voyage, he arrives in England on the eleventh of June, in the year 1687, having been gone for thirty-five years.

Comment

Crusoe's last days on the island are crammed with danger and excitement. He finally escapes his long imprisonment and returns to England. Defoe fails to inform us as to the fate of the

Spaniard and Friday's father who went to seek the sixteen men saved on the island of the savages. This is an example of Defoe's poor story structure-he sometimes neglected to tie up the loose ends.

CHAPTER FORTY-THREE

Crusoe visits the woman who has been holding his money in trust. She is still alive, but his mother and father are dead and he has been excluded from his brother's and sister's gifts because they believed him to be dead. The owners of the ship he has saved from the mutineers present him with a generous gift of silver worth almost two hundred pounds.

Comment

We notice that Defoe does not give any account of Crusoe's reactions upon his return to England. Rather, the chief concern is to tell the reader the business and financial particulars of Crusoe's life. Defoe, for many years actively engaged in business, relishes the description of various legal and monetary matters.

Anxious to discover what has happened to his plantation in Brazil, he travels to Lisbon to seek information. There he meets the old captain of the ship which had first taken him up from the sea after his escape from Sallee. The captain tells Crusoe his partner is still alive, although two of the four other men who entered into the original plan to outfit the ill-fated ship Crusoe commanded are now dead. His plantation had flourished, the annual income of which had been decreed by the procurator-fiscal (the legal judge of financial matters) to be shared as follows:

one-third went to the King's revenue, and two-thirds was given to the monastery of St. Augustine. In addition, the captain himself had received money from the profits of the plantation (since he was Crusoe's legal heir); he gives Crusoe one hundred gold coins, promising to pay the remainder as soon as possible.

Crusoe writes to Brazil and in the return mail receives a long letter which makes him pale and sick. He now owns over five thousand pounds in sterling silver! He returns the hundred gold coins to the captain, releases him from all debt and pledges him and his son yearly pensions for life. He also sends money to the widow in England and to two of his sisters.

CHAPTER FORTY-FOUR

Afraid to return by sea to England, Crusoe sets out by land to Calais. With Friday, five fellow travelers and six servants, Crusoe makes his way to Pampeluna. From there on the 15th of November, they leave for France.

A snow storm halts the progress of the travelers for a day and a night. Finally they continue. Late one afternoon, three wolves and a bear rush out of the woods. Two wolves leap at the guide. Friday shoots one dead; the other flees. The sound of the pistol shot causes the air to become filled with the howling of many wolves.

Crusoe and the others watch with great amusement as Friday entices the bear to follow him up a tall tree. Friday climbs out on a long limb. The bear follows slowly but is fearful, lest his weight break the branch. Friday nimbly swings down on the bending branch until it reaches the ground; then he waits for the bear to slowly descend. Just as the bear is about to put his hind foot on the ground, Friday shoots him in the head.

The group continues their journey, coming to a dangerous plain surrounded by woods on every side. The men must pass through a narrow lane to get through the wood. Beyond it lies the village where they are to lodge. They see a dozen wolves picking the bones of a dead horse. Half way across the plain, the men are shocked to spy over a hundred wolves coming out of the woods and charging directly towards them. Quickly forming together, the men fire a volley at the wolves, who stop, terrified. Four are dead; many are bleeding. Remembering that wolves are terrified by the voice of a man, Crusoe tells everyone to shout. At this, many of the wolves turn away; a second volley puts them into full retreat into the woods.

The men ride on, but are soon attacked again, this time by three hundred wolves. The men hide behind some fallen trees and ward off the furious charges of the wolves. Sixty wolves are slain and the victorious party finally arrives safely in the village. From there Crusoe continues his journey safely, finally arriving in England in January.

Crusoe sells his share of the Brazilian plantation. He marries and has three children. His wife dying, he ends his narrative by suggesting that his inclination to travel later led him to seek new adventures: "But these things, with some very surprising incidents in some new adventures of my own, for ten years more, I shall give a farther account hereafter."

Comment

Defoe wrote a sequel to this novel called *The Farther Adventures of Robinson Crusoe*. Since he probably planned the second novel while finishing the first, he has Crusoe suggest that more adventures are to come. Defoe's third volume about Crusoe, *The Serious Reflections of Robinson Crusoe* unlike the second is a moralizing tome with virtually no action.

ROBINSON CRUSOE

CHARACTER ANALYSES

ROBINSON CRUSOE

One of the most unusual of fictional characters, Crusoe possesses many of the contradictions one finds in every man. He is a most adventurous person but has an extremely conservative, cautious side also. Against the advice of his father, and his better judgment, he agrees to go to sea, risking his life continually even after narrow escapes from shipwreck and pirates. Yet, once upon his island, he takes pains to protect himself from the wild beasts and the elements. He sleeps in a tree the first night, then proceeds carefully to carve a comfortable existence for himself out of the wild.

At first sight, the clue of Crusoe's character may be: "It was in vain to sit still and wish for what was not to be had, and this extremity rouz'd my application." Crusoe is extremely practical. He salvages everything of value from the shipwreck, overlooking nothing which may prove useful. He knows he will probably be forced to live on the island for a long period of time, so he quickly builds a home and sets in motion a series of plans to insure his safety and comfort. He learns how to plant and reap grain, how to bake, how to make pottery and pots. His powers of observation and deduction are shown in his first encounter with the goats on the island, when he had to figure a way to kill them for food, and at the same time not frighten the whole herd away. His physical strength and industry are shown in the long months he works cutting trees and making planks; the construction of his "castle" and his summer home, and the making of several boats are also examples of his industry.

Crusoe's ingenuity, and courage can be seen not only in his work on the island but in the daring plans of escape which he executes. Crusoe is strikingly complete in character, though there are many subjects which he never discusses. Yet, this does not detract from his completeness, because he does report in such detail that we can surmise his attitude on the others. His rationality and complete awareness of a situation is illustrated by his recognition of the necessity of taking everything he might need from the shipwreck. Also, it is illustrated by his method- and the deduction he employed in arriving at that method-of hunting goats for food.

Indifferent about religion as a young man, Crusoe is led to become a devout Christian as a result of his suffering. He reads the Bible daily, and interprets his misfortune as God's will. Throughout the early part of the journal, Crusoe attempts to show the reader the influence of Divine Providence in his life. His essential seriousness is seldom relieved, however, with a sense of the incongruity of his position. The only time that humor appears in his character is when he tells of his poor attempts to make earthenware and his appreciation of Friday's clowning with the bear on their trip through France.

Crusoe's indifference to money throughout the major part of the journal is somewhat in contrast with his great attention to financial matters when he returns. His gifts to the many people who were loyal to his interests reveal his essentially generous and compassionate nature.

Crusoe is marooned on the island for twenty-seven years, two months and nineteen days. It is because we follow Crusoe's experiences from day to day and year to year, with the dates given, that we believe the impossible events which take place. One of the reasons why we accept the story as being true is because Defoe focuses, not on the island and its possible dangers, but upon the man and what he does to survive. Crusoe is truly a heroic being-a man who is in control of what he is doing, by dominating nature.

FRIDAY

A savage snatched from death by his benefactor, this strong young native becomes the devoted servant, protector, disciple and friend of Crusoe. He has great physical strength, and can easily outswim and outrun his savage pursuers. He leads the mutineers on such an exhausting trip through the island that the fatigued men are easily captured by Crusoe and the Captain's men.

Through the example and teaching of Crusoe, Friday embraces Christianity and becomes, as Crusoe tells us, a model Christian. His natural charitable and loyal nature is revealed in the devoted service he gives to Crusoe and the tears of joy he sheds at the discovery of his father. His sense of humor is shown in the funny **episode** with the bear. He begs Crusoe not to shoot the bear, for he wants to make his master and the other travelers laugh at his outwitting of the animal. Most readers will agree with Crusoe that Friday is one of the most "agreeable" persons he has ever met; he is also one of the most delightful characters in English fiction.

CRUSOE'S FATHER

A serious, practical-minded and authoritarian man, who wishes his son to put aside his desire for travel to enter the steady and sober life of middle-class business. It is Crusoe's father who tells the reader of Defoe's belief in the superiority of the middle class because of the lack of temptation to deny God.

FRIDAY'S FATHER

Saved from death by Crusoe and Friday, he courageously sets out on a journey in a boat with the Spaniard. He is an elderly, reserved and much respected member of his tribe.

THE SPANIARD

Saved with Friday's father, he pledges to bring aid to sixteen men living on the island from which the savages have come. He and Friday's father leave for the island in a boat but their fate is never recounted. One is tempted to believe that Defoe merely forgot about their situation.

XURY

He is the young boy who swears allegiance to Crusoe in his escape from Sallee. Crusoe sells him to the captain of the ship which rescued him.

THE MOOR

The wealthy pirate from whom Crusoe finally escapes in a daring plan.

MR. WELLS

A Portuguese of Lisbon, born of English parents, he becomes Crusoe's partner in their Brazilian plantation.

THE WIDOW

She is the wife of the sea captain who had befriended Crusoe early in his career. Crusoe entrusts the widow with his savings before leaving England. Thirty-five years later, he is able to show his gratitude for her husband's kind treatment of him by a generous gift to her.

THE CAPTAIN OF THE ENGLISH SHIP

A courageous and sincere gentleman, he endures the loss of his ship to the mutineers, but has the satisfaction of seeing the restoration of order and the safe return of his ship through the efforts of Crusoe, who is also responsible for saving his life.

WILL ATKINS

One of the mutineers who is forgiven by the English captain.

ROBINSON

A mutineer who helps the captain regain control of his ship.

THE PORTUGUESE CAPTAIN

He saves Crusoe and Xury from the sea, buys the boy from him and lives to tell Crusoe, years later, of the events which occurred during his captivity on the island.

ROBINSON CRUSOE

CRITICAL COMMENTARY

The middle-class reading public in eighteenth-century England devoured with great relish travel, escape, and adventure books. Defoe's library, for example, contained all the important books of travel, such as Richard Hakluyt's, *Voyages*; Dampier's, *New Voyage Around the World*; Robert Knox's, *Historical Relation of Ceylon*; and Captain Woodes Roger's, *Cruising Voyage Around the World*, which included an account of Alexander Selkirk. The latter was a Scottish sailor who later published an account of his life on the Pacific island (one of the Juan Fernandez group) where he had lived, marooned, for four years. It was Selkirk's situation that Defoe has expounded upon, in fictional form. When he published *The Life and Strange Surprising Adventures of Robinson Crusoe, of York, Mariner* in 1719, Defoe's reading public, for the most part, assumed that it also was a true journal. Since many religious readers refused to read fiction because it was a "lie," Defoe had to be able to convince his readers of Crusoe's reality.

Perhaps the appeal of the novel lies in the fact that it deals with the impossible, but at the same time, it is very realistic. We are asked to share the varied **episodes** of storms, pirate attacks, an escape from slavery, shipwrecks, cannibalistic horrors, violent deaths, war with mutinous sailors, and the attacks of five hundred savage wolves. We accept the unreality of the experience, sufficiently thrilled by the excitement Defoe is able to generate and unwilling to criticize harshly his dependence on mere incident to arrest our interest.

Realistic description pervades the book. Lionel Stevenson, in discussing the popular appeal of the book in *The English Novel: A Panorama*, observes, "It was a story of wild adventure and yet it was told with the coolness of everyday routine. No other **theme**, perhaps, has as strong a psychological impact as the struggle of an individual to survive in hostile surroundings. By the simple device of telling it in the first person, Defoe gave an incomparable sense of actuality. The narrator was such an average unimaginative specimen of humanity that most readers identified themselves with him completely and automatically before they finished the first chapter. Matter-of-fact tradesmen and artisans, approving all Crusoe's efficient contrivances, reveled vicariously in his triumph over primitive hardships, and perhaps secretly envied him for his remoteness from the counter and the workbench."

Defoe was very careful about staying within the bounds of the ordinary, having already made the reader believe the fantastic situation on the island, by making his hero "life size." By life size we mean that the ordinary man could do the things Crusoe did to stay alive on the island. A critic pointed out that Crusoe "arrives at no excellence ... the carpentering, tailoring, pottery, etc., are all just what will answer his purpose ... Crusoe rises only to the point to which all men may be made to feel they might."

Defoe wrote in what is loosely called the "picaresque" tradition, whereby the hero of the story leads a life of adventure-

depending on his wits for his survival. In true picaresque, the **protagonist** moves from one social stratum to another, or from one professional class to another, the object of the change being diversified social exposé or **satire**. It is in this respect that Defoe differed from his contemporaries, such as Jonathan Swift. Defoe's works deal with biography, voyage literature and morality-not a conscious exposé of the evils of the time.

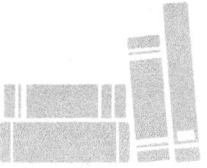

ROBINSON CRUSOE

ESSAY QUESTIONS AND ANSWERS

Question: Discuss the importance of *Robinson Crusoe* in the development of the novel genre.

Answer: Since *Robinson Crusoe* was one of the earliest novels written in the seventeenth century (1719), its position in the chronology of English literature development, quite aside from its intrinsic merit, is of some worth; most particularly, however, it is important as an influence upon other novels. Defoe possessed to a rare degree the gift of bringing verisimilitude (the appearance of truth) to his writing. In his early prose pamphlets and particularly in his realistic-like account of the apparition of Mrs. Veal, he exhibited those qualities of careful description and credibility in detail to convince readers of the "authenticity" of his works. In *Robinson Crusoe*, Defoe had to overcome the attitude of many readers, whose religious scruples forbade their reading of fiction. Fiction was untrue, so what profit could it bring to a reader concerned with truth? Defoe circumvented this kind of reader opposition by publishing the book as if it were the true account of *Robinson Crusoe* of York, a mariner. And he succeeded eminently in making readers believe that Crusoe was a real person. In every great novel of the many which followed *Robinson Crusoe*, authors such as Henry Fielding, Oliver Goldsmith, Sir Walter Scott, and Charles Dickens, following Defoe's approach, were able to create characters realistic speech and action are unforgettable.

Question: What kind of novel is *Robinson Crusoe*?

Answer: Clearly, the novel is a realistic adventure story, written in the form of the picaresque tradition. It is an autobiography of a young man who throws all warnings aside to lead a life of adventure on the high seas. Crusoe narrates to the reader all that happens to him and how he reacts to the situations at hand. The novel is full of realistic description, which makes the story believable.

The novel is called "adventurous" because of Defoe's heavy use of incident and suspense throughout. The hero, Robinson Crusoe, is involved in a series of exciting episodes. We witness a series of melodramatic incidents: there are numerous storms, shipwrecks, an earthquake, violent battles with savages and mutineers, and a harrowing escape from wolves.

Question: Is Robinson Crusoe a hero?

Answer: Yes, in the context of the story, Robinson Crusoe is a hero. But, one must understand that a hero is one who alters situations in a story, he brings about a change for the good. He helps the damsel in distress, and he goes off to war for the purpose of fighting a good cause. Robinson Crusoe has things happen to him, which are not planned-he is constantly reacting to events brought about by outside forces. Crusoe reacts heroically because he does something about his situation, but he never is the instigator of an action until he is put into a situation by Providence, where he has to act, or lose his life. It is the manner in which Crusoe reacts that makes him heroic. He is very courageous about changing his own situation, when the need arises. But, other than that, he is not in control of his destiny.

Question: What place does Divine Providence have in the novel?

Answer: Defoe's belief that everything is directed by God is carried out in the novel. Crusoe is deluged by storms, enslaved by Turkish pirates, and eventually imprisoned on a lonely island. Crusoe is constantly reacting to events which are beyond his control. He is like an empty barrel being tossed about the sea. By Crusoe's own belief every event that takes place is an act of Providence. The events which take place in the story are punishment to Crusoe because of his initial sin of leaving his proper station in life. His final rescue from the island is God's reward to him because of his total conversion to Christianity.

Question: Explain the reasoning behind Defoe's belief that the middle class is superior to other classes.

Answer: The middle class is the class most suited to the human state of happiness because one does not have an excess of wealth, thus becoming decadent and denying the word of God, or one does not have too little wealth to create a disbelief, and "take the name of my God in vain."

BIBLIOGRAPHY

Defoe's literary and journalistic output runs to over four hundred titles. The most important works are listed in the *Cambridge History of English Literature*, Vol. II, (495-514).

BIOGRAPHIES

Fitzgerald, Brian. *Daniel Defoe*, 1954.

Freeman, W. The *Incredible Defoe*, 1950.

Lee, William. *Life and Recently Discovered Writings*, 3 Vol., 1869.

Sutherland, James R. *Defoe*, 1937.

Trent, William P. *Daniel Defoe: How to Know Him*, 1916.

Watson, Francis. *Daniel Defoe*, 1952.

Wright, Thomas. *Life*, 1931.

CRITICISM

Baker, Ernest. *The English Novel*, Vol. III, 1930.

Baugh, Albert C. and others. *A Literary History of England*, 1948.

Church, R. *The Growth of the English Novel*, 1951.

Dobree, Bonamy. "Some Aspects of Defoe's Prose," in *Pope and His Contemporaries*, 1949.

Halewood, William H. "Religion and Invention in *Robinson Crusoe*." *Essays in Criticism*, XIV, 339-351, 1963.

Stevenson, Lionel. *The English Novel*, 1960.

Watt, Ian. *The Rise of the Novel*, 1960.

Woolf, Virginia. *The Common Reader*, 1932.

COLLECTIONS OF DEFOE'S NOVELS

Aitken, George A., ed. *Romances and Narratives*, vol. 16, 1895.

Maynadier, Gustavus H., ed. *Novels and Selected Writings*, vol. 14, 1927-8.

LETTERS

Healey, George H. *The Letters of Daniel Defoe*, 1955.

www.ingramcontent.com/pod-product-compliance
Lightning Source LLC
LaVergne TN
LVHW011737060526
838200LV00051B/3204